D0900015

OLD SPODE CHINA

John Bedford

WALKER AND COMPANY
NEW YORK

Library of Congress Catalog Card Number: 72-84598

First published in the United States of America in 1969 by Walker and Company, a division of the Walker Publishing Company, Inc.

Printed in Hong Kong

Contents

Introduction

'Old Spode' has always been a firm favourite with the lover of English china; and it makes new friends with every generation.

It also has a special historical interest, in that Josiah Spode II is generally credited with the invention of English bone china—that beautiful and still-flourishing hybrid into which merged the 'hard-paste' porcelains of the Far East and the Continent and the 'soft-pastes' of the eighteenth-century English and French factories.

Bone china was not, of course, the only Spode production. Before it came along the firm had been making fine stonewares and earthenwares in the Staffordshire tradition; and later on Josiah Spode II was to reach a wider market with his felspar porcelain and stone china. The Spode story would not be complete, therefore, without some account of

Red stoneware jug with applied reliefs in black. Mark SPODE impressed. (Victoria & Albert Museum.)

both these wares. Since, however, they were all made over a very long period I have found it difficult to relate the photographs to the text. The reader may therefore find it more helpful to pursue the story in the text first after which there should be no difficulty in finding one's way among the illustrations.

The author wishes to express his grateful thanks to Mr Harold Holdway, Art Director of W. T. Copeland & Sons Ltd for reading the manuscript; and to Mr R. J. Charleston, Keeper of the Department of Ceramics at the Victoria and Albert Museum, London, for allowing monochrome and colour photographs of pieces in the Museum's collection to be taken especially for this book.

Crater-shaped vase in red stoneware with white 'sacrifices' relief in the Wedgwood manner. Mark SPODE impressed. (Victoria & Albert Museum.)

1. Josiah the First:

(a) Earthenwares and Stonewares

At the opening of the eighteenth century the collection of towns in North Staffordshire which we now know as the Potteries was a string of villages, hamlets and lone farms connected by lanes and tracks, most of them accessible only by packhorse. A map of the times shows that, scattered throughout the area, but mainly concentrated around the only township, Burslem, some forty to fifty small potbanks raised their conical tops among the farmhouses and cottages. The district was well suited to the potter's trade. 'For making their different sorts of pots,' wrote Dr Thomas Plot in 1686 in his *History of Staffordshire*, 'they have as many different sorts of clay, which they dig round about the towne, all within half a mile's distance, the best being found nearest the coale . . .'

These clays yielded the potters cloudy, mottled, red or black bodies, also the friable 'slips' used to decorate the wares. Apart from earthenwares, they made the harder brown and buff stonewares which, a generation earlier, the Dutch brothers Elers had supplied to the London market in competition with the little red teapots coming in from China and the Low Countries. These wares they made and fired to such temperatures that, even in these country lanes, 'the smoke and vapours from the ovens entering the atmosphere produced that dense white cloud which from about eight o'clock till twelve on the Saturday morning [the time of 'firing up' as it was called] so completely enveloped the whole interior of the town, as to cause persons often to run against each other, travellers·to mistake the road: and strangers have mentioned it as extremely disagreeable, and not unlike the smoke of Etna and Vesuvius.'

The wares included large and small dishes, mugs and jugs, cream piggins, novelties such as toy cradles for marriage gifts and money boxes for the pennies of the town apprentices; also a great many butter pots. These were long cylindrical affairs made to carry butter from the dairy farms of Staffordshire and Derbyshire to the great market at Uttoxeter, where the London butter merchants and cheesemongers had their 'factorages', and if they brought fame to Burslem they also brought some notoriety. By Act of Parliament the pots had to be of such a size as to carry exactly fourteen pounds; and apparently the Burslem potters—or some of them at all events—were not averse from using here some of the tricks they had learnt in making secret channels and false entries for puzzle jugs and fuddling cups. Dr Plot tells us, in fact, that special measures had to be taken to check up on the methods of 'these little Moorlandish cheats (than whom no people whatever are esteemed more subtile)' as he rather unkindly commented. The butter factors had to keep in the market all the summer a surveyor, 'who, if he have ground to suspect any of the *Pots*, tryes them with an instrument of Iron, made like a *Cheese-Taster*, only larger and longer, called an *Auger*, or *Butter-boare*, with which he makes proof (thrusting it in *obliquely*) to the Bottom of the Pot . . .'

Pastille burner in red stoneware, with dark brown classical reliefs, standing upon three dolphins. (Victoria & Albert Museum.)

Some of the potting families had been living around Burslem since Elizabethan or even mediaeval days, and their names have a familiar ring even today. There were five different Wedgwoods, two Daniels, two Adamses, as well as Warburtons, Bagnalls, Woods, Mayers and Stevensons. Fifty years later, another list gives us other names well known to modern collectors—Astbury, Whieldon, Malkin, Heath, Clowes, Booth.

Between these dates, in fact, something like a revolution had occurred in the Pottery. The fine white Chinese porcelain and the Dutch and English delftwares had set Staffordshire on its mettle, and the potters went as far afield as Devon and Dorset for finer clays, also adding flint in the 'mix' for strength, developing fine lead glazes to carry rich colours on their earthenwares, and adopting all manner of new working techniques. In the space of twenty-seven years—from 1722 to 1749—no fewer than nine separate patents were taken out for new processes or the use of new materials.

Some of these patents led to vigorous quarrels among the potters. In 1733 one Ralphe Shawe, for example, tried to restrain the others from using a process which he claimed as his own invention, but which had actually been introduced by John Astbury some years before: the resultant proceedings are described thus in Ward's *Burslem Dialogue*:

Terrick. Dust moind, Rafe, owt o' th' treyal at Staffurt o' Johnny Mutchil for makkin Rafy Shay's patten ware?
Leigh. Oi just remember, bu' oi wur ony a big lad at th' teyme. It had bin mitch tawkt abaht, and when it wur oer, they aw toud'n wat th' judge sed to th' mesters—'Gooa whomm, potters, an mak wot soourts o' pots yoa loiken.' An when they coom to Boslem, aw th' bells i' Hoositon, an Stooke, an th' tahn, wurn ringin loike hey-go-mad, aw th' dey.

A wise judge—and a great day for the Potteries.

Among the names of the master potters given above, however, a famous one is still missing. The owner of it was not yet a master and to find it one has to look at an entry made in a memorandum book in the year 1749 by perhaps the most celebrated potter of them all, Thomas Whieldon, of Little Fenton. The entry runs as follows:

		£	s.	d.
April 9	Hired Siah Spoade, to give him from this time to Martelmas next 2s. 3d. or 2s. 6d. if he Deserves it			
	2d year	0.	2.	9.
	3d year	0.	3.	3.
	Pd full earnest	0.	1.	0.

The young man who thus hired himself out was Josiah Spode, son of a Josiah Spode of Lane Delph. He was at this time sixteen years old, and had doubtless already served three or four years with some other potter—turning handles, working treadles, standing saggars in the kilns.

Josiah must have given his new employer every satisfaction, for at the end of the three-year term we find another entry in the master potter's book:

		£	s.	d.
1752 Feby. 22	Hired Josiah Spoad for next Martelmas, per week	0.	7.	0.
	I am to give him earn.	0.	5.	0.
	Pd. in part	0.	1.	0.
	Pd. do.	0.	4.	0.

Two years later there had perhaps come into the young journeyman's mind the idea of moving on, for we find that in the next agreement made, his employer, putting his wages up to 7s. 6d., paid him the unusually high 'earnest' of £1 11s. 6d. The money was needed, for by now Josiah was a married man, and the father of a son—again named Josiah, in the family tradition.

Josiah Spode I's signature on a bill from Mountford and Spode to Josiah Wedgwood & Co.

Bill from Spode's London warehouse in Portugal Street, Lincoln's Inn Fields.

Coffee pot in red stoneware with 'Egyptian' reliefs in black. Mark SPODE impressed. (Victoria & Albert Museum.)

At this time Thomas Whieldon, his employer, stood in the very front rank of the Staffordshire master potters. He had set up in business on his own in 1740, taking a small range of low thatched buildings. There he made his agate knife hafts for the Sheffield cutlers and snuff boxes for the Birmingham hardwaremen, who would fit them with metal loops, hinges and springs for the shopmen in the towns. His beginnings must have been very modest indeed, for in his early days he is said to have himself carried his wares to the tradesmen in a basket.

By the time Josiah Spode came to work for him, however, Whieldon was making most types of Staffordshire wares of the day. Apart from the famous agate wares in variegated colours, there was the well-known range of tortoiseshell table wares, also creamwares, black basaltes and black-glazed wares. In the same year that 'Siah' Spode got his large advance, Whieldon had entered into partner-ship with another enterprising young man, named Josiah Wedgwood, who had been working for him for some years: one result of this association was the famous Wedgwood green-glazed wares, after which this other Josiah went to Burslem—to found his own pottery-village at Etruria and to earn world-wide fame. Whieldon also made a fortune, became Sheriff of the County, and died full of honour and years in 1798. He lies buried, among other famous master potters, in Stoke churchyard.

Josiah Spode seems to have stayed on with Whieldon as a journeyman potter until about 1762, for he next appears as manager of a pottery at Stoke. This was owned by a partner-ship between a William Banks—who was perhaps not himself a potter—and that famous John Turner whom we distinguish from other potters of the name by the qualifica-tion 'of Lane End'—for it was to a pottery in that place that he moved on to make a fortune and a name. At the Banks and Turner potworks the principal product was creamware and also the fine white stonewares which had been de-veloped by John Turner. Banks seems to have retired from the business by about 1771, leaving Josiah as a master potter, but continuing for some time in partnership with others. For example, from that year we find accounts rendered to the firm of Josiah and Thomas Wedgwood at Shelton for wares—perhaps sold 'in the white' for painting—made by 'Spode & Tomkinson'. This latter was a solicitor who may have been a sleeping partner providing the new master

12

potter with much-needed capital. Another invoice of three years later shows Josiah in association with one of the Mountfords. In fact in 1772 he had entered into a co-partnership with Thomas Mountford, 'gentleman of Newcastle-under-Lyme', to engage in 'the art and mystery of Pot making and in selling, bartering and transporting all sorts of pots and earthenware for the space of seven years . . .' This indenture, which is printed in full in T. G. Cannon's *Old Spode*, promises to instruct Mountford 'in the whole art and mystery of the aforesaid trade of a potter as far as the knowledge of the said Josiah Spode there extends'. In return for this Mountford was to pay into the partnership the sum of £500 'to be laid out in the purchase of such clay, flint, lead colours, pots, potboards and other wood wares, utensils and things incident or belonging to the said trade'. By its terms Josiah was allowed to continue his arrangement with Tomlinsons, and it was also not to affect 'the business of a Haberdasher' carried on by his wife —apparently both sides of the Spode family were hard workers. One of the witnesses to the deed was Spode's old employer Thomas Whieldon, whose signature appears on it.

By 1776, however, when he was in his forty-third year, Josiah had established himself firmly in business, for in that

Flower holder basket and cover in buff stoneware with white reliefs of putti, classical scrolls and acanthus leaves. (Victoria & Albert Museum.)

year he purchased the potworks—perhaps the haberdasher's business helped in raising the capital.

From the catalogue of a number of early pieces (which were destroyed by fire at an exhibition at the Alexandra Palace in 1873) we learn that Josiah I's chief production at this time was a fine stoneware of the type which had been made at the factory by John Turner, having white reliefs on chocolate or buff grounds. The Works Museum still possesses moulds which were used for these relief decorations: some have Turner's name scratched on them, some Spode's. There is also a series with Turner's name impressed in capitals: these are thought to have been bought later on by the works when John Turner died at Lane End at the early age of forty-eight—a great loss to English potting. The epitaph given him—'Below lies one whose name is traced in sand' was not entirely appropriate, for in fact he has left his name and his instinct for fine potting on some of the finest wares ever to be made in Staffordshire—and no doubt passed on a great deal of his skill to the manager who succeeded him at Stoke.

The subjects of these moulds vary a good deal, and in fact give us a very fair idea of the cross-currents of decorative motifs which were passed around from pottery to pottery at that time. There are the classical themes—putti, goddesses, 'sacrifices'—all very familiar from the work of Wedgwood and the Adamses: there are also some very spirited genre subjects—convivial gatherings of drinkers and smokers, hunting subjects, rural views with horses at plough. Even our old friend Toby Fillpot, taken from a print by Dighton, appears on one of these moulds: it is illustrated in another book in this series.*

Among the other wares made at this time were the 'black basaltes' which Wedgwood had developed from the old 'Egyptian black'. of Whieldon and the other earlier potters, also red and buff wares of various kinds. The production of creamwares also continued. It might be said, in fact, that

*Toby Jugs, by John Bedford.

the range of wares turned out at this time represented a fair cross-section of the commercial products of the Staffordshire potteries of the day. Not for them the hazards of the luxury porcelain trade—Chelsea and Bow had already gone, and Lowestoft was soon to follow. Josiah I had worked his way up from journeyman, and from first to last the Spodes at Stoke—like the Wedgwoods at Etruria—were to combine fine potting with business acumen. Both factories made sure that the public knew who had made their fine wares, for they imprinted their family names simply and grandly on their pieces—as much as to say that there was only one Wedgwood and there was only one Spode.

As already noted, however, there *was* another Spode, even another Josiah Spode. This was the first Josiah's son, and at the time when his father became proprietor of the Stoke works he was twenty-two years old. Henceforward, therefore, to distinguish between father and son at Stoke we may treat them as heads of State, thus: Josiah I (1733–1797) and Josiah II (1754–1827). It is not at all inappropriate to do this, for within the small kingdom of the growing potyard they were indeed ruling monarchs.

Cream jug in brown stoneware, painted in colours. Mark SPODE impressed. (Victoria & Albert Museum.)

Inkstand in buff stoneware, with white reliefs. Mark SPODE impressed. (Victoria & Albert Museum.)

'*Parrot*' *pattern on network ground.*

'*Tumbledown Dick*' *pattern on a* '*cracked ice*' *ground.*

The '*Blue Italian*' *pattern, from a coffee-cup, flattened out to give an* '*all-around*' *view.*

1. Josiah the First:

(b) Bone China

For the collector of English china the years around the turn of the eighteenth and the nineteenth centuries must always be of the deepest interest. The porcelains in use during the eighteenth century—the foreign 'hard-pastes' and the English and French 'soft-pastes'—hitherto quite separate streams, now converged, and it was during the two decades lying on either side of the year 1800 that there came into existence that admirable hybrid known as English bone china—virtually the same material which most of the English-speaking countries use for their table wares today.

Beginnings of this kind are always interesting to the connoisseur. Sprimont's efforts with the delightfully errant early Chelsea paste are in many ways more charming and attractive than the full perfection of the later Gold Anchor period; while Bristol Worcester's quaint and sketchy 'smoky primitive' printed wares have more charm than the fully evolved ones of the Hancock–Holdship partnership (if that is what it was) at Dr Wall's Worcester.

So far as bone china is concerned the first Spodes, father and son, were in at the very beginning of this beginning: they may even have been the very first ones to make it, so it may be rewarding to look at the story in some detail.

Down to about the year 1790 the situation in English ceramics was that a number of quite different porcelain bodies existed, only one (or possibly two) of which bore any resemblance to the kind which had been imported for the past two hundred years from, first, the Far East, mainly China, and latterly from Meissen and (very recently) Sèvres. That one known true, or hard-paste English porcelain had been in production at the New Hall factory, Shelton, in Staffordshire, for the last nine years.

This New Hall porcelain (or 'real china' as its makers proudly called it) had come into being as the result of the probings of a Quaker wholesale chemist of Plymouth by the name of William Cookworthy. Somewhere in the 1740s he had been reading some letters written by a Jesuit missionary who lived in the great Chinese porcelain-making city of Ching-te-chen, where, as he related in one place, more than a million souls lived and over three thousand kiln fires blazed night and day.

The French priest had given in some detail an account of the materials and methods used in making the Chinese porcelain, and these had been rediscovered in Germany at the beginning of the century, quite independently, by the young alchemist Johann Friedrich Böttger, working at Meissen for the Elector of Saxony.

Cookworthy would obviously have known of this fact, but it interested him to discover if the same kind of porcelain could be made with native English materials. Eventually he found them—two forms of felspathic rock known to the Chinese as *kaolin* and *petuntse*—in the china stone and china clay of his native West Country: actually at Tregonning Hill, near Helston.

Before this discovery, of course, the English and French factories, being ignorant of the Chinese and German secrets, had been making porcelain of a sort from such materials as crushed glass, white clay, soapstone and bone ash, each type varying with the particular factory—links existing between Chelsea and Derby, Bow and Lowestoft, Worcester and Caughley, with Liverpool as a mixture of pretty well everything. Something very like this 'soft-paste' had also been made, even earlier, at such French factories as Chantilly, Vincennes and Sèvres. There had been improvements both in materials and the handling of them, but down to the 1760s there had substantially been no great changes.

In the year 1768 however, Cookworthy, having worked out a technique for using the local china stone and china clay, took out a patent for covering both his methods and materials, and began to make the wares now known to collectors as 'Cookworthy's Plymouth'. During the next few years he became associated with a young Bristol merchant named Richard Champion; and about 1770 the factory was moved to Bristol, presumably so as to be nearer to a good market for the wares. In 1773, Cookworthy decided to retire from business, and sold his patent to Champion.

The next milestone in the story occurred two years later, in 1775, when Champion applied for an extension until 1796 of his newly acquired patent. His motive was obviously to ensure that if, as the result of Cookworthy's pioneering, it became possible to make porcelain of the Chinese and continental type in England from English materials, then whoever had the exclusive right to use these materials would obviously accumulate a huge fortune, either by making the porcelain itself or by selling the materials to other potters. One of the owners of land rich in china stone and china clay was Thomas Pitt, later Lord Camelford: he became one of the partners in Champion's enterprise, and told a friend that he had been informed (presumably by

Teapot in cane-coloured ware ('caneware') with floral applied reliefs. Mark SPODE impressed. (Victoria & Albert Museum.)

Champion) that 'he might expect to get £100,000 a year by the business'.

The enterprising (but in fact, doomed) Champion proceeded to back up his claim by tactics that have been used all down the centuries. He made presents of Bristol china (now known to collectors as 'Champion's Bristol') to Lady North, wife of the Prime Minister, and to the Duchess of Portland, whose husband was also one of his patrons; he even managed to obtain an audience of Queen Charlotte herself, at which he presented her with two medallions representing the King and herself in high relief—whereupon her Majesty (who had only recently appointed Josiah Wedgwood as her Potter) promised the Bristolian her 'protection'.

As soon as Champion petitioned for extension ('enlargement' was the word used) of his patent, the Staffordshire potters, led by Josiah Wedgwood, combined their interests and strenuously opposed Champion's representations. They needed the Cornish materials for their earthenwares and stonewares, and certainly did not want to be forbidden either from competing with Champion in making translucent porcelain, or in being denied the materials for use in making their own products. Their tactics were every bit as ingenious as Champion's: when his Bill came up in the Lords, Josiah Wedgwood wrote to the landowning peers pointing out how injurious it would be to them if, by limiting sales to Champion, 'materials of great value should be locked up in the bowels of the earth'.

There is not space here to tell the full story of this fight—which at times almost took on a 'cloak and sword' flavour (including all-night rides from Bristol to London)—but eventually it fell out that while Champion would be allowed to extend his exclusive right to the use of the materials in the manufacture of 'translucent porcelain', the earthenware makers were permitted to use it for their opaque earthenwares and stonewares.

The New Hall enterprise continued making its hard-

Earthenware plate, printed in blue with the 'Lucano' pattern, taken from an aquatint of 1798 of the Bridge of Lucano, near Rome. Mark SPODE 16 and B twice printed in blue. (Victoria & Albert Museum.)

Earthenware plate printed with an engraving in the 'Caramanian' series: 'Sarcophagi and Sepulchres at the head of the harbour at Cacamo.' The border vignettes are from the 'Indian Sporting' series. Mark SPODE and 28 impressed.

paste for another decade—and this again is another story. What will interest us now, however, is to see how both the soft-paste porcelain makers—like Duesbury of Derby and Martin Barr of Worcester—and also the earthenware makers of Staffordshire, began now to see the possibilities of the Cornish materials in improving their own wares. In the very forefront of the Staffordshire men stood Josiah Spode I.

The Act 'enlarging' Champion's patent had hardly got on to the Statute Book, in fact, before the potters were in Cornwall inspecting the materials which Cookworthy had found and tried. They could not actually copy Champion's formula, but, as Josiah Wedgwood had pointed out during the recent controversy, 'no distinct line has ever been drawn between porcelain and earthenware'. And although Champion had an exclusive contract with landowners like Camelford for the supply of the materials, Wedgwood had

Earthenware plate printed in blue with a version of the 'Willow' pattern. Mark 'SPODE' impressed and a cross printed in blue. (Victoria & Albert Museum.)

also been careful to suggest that Champion's specification would very likely fail with his porcelain. This specification, he claimed, was 'a lighthouse teaching the trade precisely what they are to avoid': no doubt Champion had deliberately falsified it. From then onwards, at all events, the Cornish landowners sold their materials to anyone who wanted to buy them; and after a year or two in association with the New Hall enterprise—to whom he now sold his patent—Champion, a ruined man, passes out of ceramic history and to an early death in America.

One of the first of the wares to be improved by making use of the new Cornish materials was Wedgwood's own cream-ware—'Queen's ware' as he had called it after his elevation to the rank of Queen's Potter. This had been a development of the traditional Staffordshire materials used from the beginning of the century; and now, by using Cornish stone alongside the Staffordshire flint and clay, it became a formidable competitor to the older wares in the world's market, even to porcelain itself. Other Staffordshire men used the materials: so too did the rival factories of Derby and Worcester, where the English soft-paste body had reached a high standard of perfection but was still expensive to make.

We must turn aside to look at what was happening at this time at the Spode works, which by now occupied a considerable area at the junction of the turnpike road and the lane from Shelton to Newcastle. It lay at the southern end of the whole Pottery, and in fact was the first to be seen by the traveller from London.

There had been a great expansion in the business of the pottery. In 1770, Josiah I had installed a beam steam engine, one of the first men in the Pottery to do so. By 1785, he had got to the stage where he could afford a London warehouse and showroom, like those maintained by Wedgwood, Worcester and Caughley. He had come into contact with a certain William Copeland, a member of an old Staffordshire potting family who by trade was

23

either a traveller or a warehouseman in the tea trade. As their businesses were not at all unrelated—china wares were often imported by the tea merchant—it was decided that Copeland would open a warehouse in Fore Street, Cripplegate, at the northern end of the City, where the Spode wares could be displayed and offered for sale to the London 'china-men'. It may have been this connection with the tea trade, and familiarity with the wares coming in from China as well as the painted 'tea-papers' in which the commodity was wrapped, that at a time when many potters were turning to the classical, gave the firm that strong predilection for oriental themes which it never entirely lost.

It seems that Josiah II had already been established in London even before the opening of the warehouse there, for his daughter Eliza was baptized in Cripplegate in 1778 and his wife died there four years later. With the opening of the warehouse; however, a separate partnership was established at the London end, with Copeland as a member.

Thus, by the late 1780s and early 1790s we have a picture of a highly successful business, founded—like so many others before and since—on the partnership of a father who had worked his way up from artisan and manager and a son who had learnt the trade under him and was keen to develop it still further. There is a parallel even in pottery with the

Earthenware jug printed in blue. Mark SPODE and four dots impressed, and a cross printed in blue. (Victoria & Albert Museum.)

24

Duesburys of Derby, one of the Spodes' chief rivals.

By this time, of course, the Spodes, like most of the other Staffordshire potters, were buying the Cornish materials to improve their earthenwares and stonewares. For their printed wares, sold in competition with the Oriental blue and white, it would obviously have been in their interests to produce as fine a body as possible. But there are now reasons to believe (which will be adduced later) that even before the '90s were out, the two Spodes—or perhaps the father on his own at Stoke, egged on by the son at the selling end in London—were experimenting with the use of the new materials in making at any rate a translucent earthenware, anticipating the day when the Champion patent, now worked by New Hall, would come to an end. Unfortunately the partnership, unlike that between Wedgwood and the merchant prince Bentley, has left behind no correspondence to tell us anything of their plans and schemes, their successes and failures—perhaps they were canny enough to destroy everything which passed between Stoke and London, in case their secrets fell into hands which could profit by them.

There was, however, every inducement to press on with the development of the finer body. In 1787 a new treaty with France had reduced the mutual duty on ceramics wares from 80% to 10%; which meant that French porcelain could now enter the country at very cheap prices. In the following year Flight of Worcester was having to send his sons to France to buy china in the white so that they could compete in the home market. On the other hand, the lower import duty meant that manufacturers of earthenware—principally Spode, Wedgwood and the other Staffordshire men—could now, with their cheaper goods, get into the French market and undercut the *faience* and porcelains made there. It also meant that there was now an even greater market in both countries for a cheaper kind of porcelain—in other words, bone china.

There is still some dispute as to who was really the first Staffordshire potter to make a successful bone china. It

Earthenware tureen and cover, printed in blue. Marks, on base SPODE and
39 impressed; on base and cover SPODE and A printed in blue. (Victoria
& Albert Museum.)

Ladle en suite with tureen, printed in blue. Mark SPODE and a lozenge
impressed C printed in blue. (Victoria & Albert Museum.)

Two knife rests printed in blue with SPODE in a cartouche.

involved taking the formula as roughly outlined by Champion (which as already mentioned seems in fact to have been faked) and substituting for some of the china stone a proportion of calcined bone ash.

This was in fact already being used by the soft-paste factories in combination with their glassy frits, but now it was to be used in much larger quantities. The formula as it eventually came out was roughly four parts of china stone, three and a half parts of china clay and six parts of bone ash. This gave a kind of hybrid porcelain, which would have many of the qualities of true hard-paste, but which could be fired in much the same way as the older and now perfected creamwares—a much more economical process than the one Champion had used in his ill-starred efforts at Bristol.

The Spodes' claim to be the first to achieve this on a workable basis rests upon the fact that in the pattern books, which are still at the Works, there are several numbered patterns, painted on paper with the watermarks of 1794 and 1795. These numbers are fairly high ones—381 in 1794 and 674 and 675 in the year 1795. Moreover, there are in existence in the Victoria and Albert Museum two dishes, formerly in the Gulson collection (a Spode family one), which bear an even earlier pattern number, 282. As it seems unlikely that the Spodes would have produced so many patterns—apart from experimental pieces—in the space of one year it does seem that they must have started at least two or three years before.

The watermark is not, of course, incontrovertible evidence, for the paper could have been bought at any time after the year in question. There are, however, other shreds of evidence that the Spodes were ready to enter the field with a 'translucent' ware at this time—some years before the expiry of Champion's patent. To begin with, there are certain events, private for the Spodes and public for the nation, which pinpoint 1794 as being a critical moment.

In that year, for example, a duty of 30% was levied on all decorated porcelain, while imports of continental porcelain were totally prohibited—except from Holland, and even here a permit was needed. This, in effect, gave a monopoly to the East India Company's imports of wares from the Far East, a circumstance of which that enterprising body took full advantage, for the price of Chinese porcelain soared in sympathy with that of the home-made variety. The French wars had been dragging on for some years, and of course, English exports to the Continent were as effectively stopped by the blockade as were continental imports into England. Several important Staffordshire potters ran into difficulty at this time—among them the sons of our old friend John Turner of Lane End.

On the face of it, then, this would seem as good a time as any to retrench, to pull in one's horns until better times arrived. But the Spodes did exactly the opposite. They moved their London warehouse from the trade quarter in the north of the City to the fashionable shopping area of Lincoln's Inn Fields, taking premises in Portugal Street. Moreover, this was no mere china and glass shop but a very large warehouse. Up till that time, in fact, it had been the Salopian China Warehouse, for it had been used by Thomas Turner of Caughley to display his wares in London. Before that it had been the Theatre Royal, Lincoln's Inn, and had drawn the town there in 1714 by opening under the manager John Rich with a performance of George Farquhar's famous and long-lived comedy *The Recruiting Officer*. John Gay's *The Beggar's Opera* had also been produced there: thus giving rise to the quip about this piece having made 'Gay rich and Rich gay'.

All this could surely mean only one thing, that in spite of difficulties—perhaps because of them, especially the shut-down of exports to the Continent—the Spodes had decided to branch out with wares they thought they could sell to the Town—who were always in a position to buy, no matter what happened to the earthenware clients. They had something to offer in competition with the now more highly priced 'Nankin wares'; and it must have been bone china.

28

Stone china dish printed in blue with a chinoiserie pattern. Mark SPODE, in a label across a simulated Chinese character above 'Stone China' printed in blue.

Detail of mark on a Stone China plate made as a copy of a Chinese plate. (Victoria & Albert Museum.)

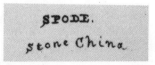

Bone china tub-shaped potpourri bowl and cover with four gilt paw feet, scroll projections on the rim. The pierced cover has a knob in the form of gilt flames. Reserved panels in a dark blue ground are painted in colours with a bird in a landscape with a bridge, with sprays of formal flowers in gold. (Victoria & Albert Museum.)

Bone china tea-cup and saucer painted with rosettes in silver lustre alternate with foliated devices in red, with gilt edges. Unmarked, but perhaps Spode. (Victoria & Albert Museum.)

Bone china hexagonal plate with small sprays and a bouquet of flowers painted in brown and red and flowers in slight relief. Mark SPODE 2089 in red. c. 1815.

Bone china plate painted in blue and gold with a pattern of shells and seaweed: the lobed rim has a filt chain-pattern border. Mark SPODE 2974 printed in red. (Victoria & Albert Museum.)

At all events, the firm continued to prosper. By 1796, according to Jewitt, the profits exceeded £13,000—a huge sum, which has to be multiplied by something like twenty-five to arrive at today's value. William Copeland, the London manager, was awarded a bonus of £1,000 and made a full partner in the London firm, which was now styled Spode, Son and Copeland. The 'son' of course, was Josiah II. It had been a remarkable feat to build such a business in twenty years; and it was only forty-four years since that 'Martelmas' when Josiah I had started with old Master Whieldon at his 2s. 3d. a week 'or 2s. 6d. if he Deserves it'.

In fact, it was the climax of Josiah I's career. In the following year—just after the Battle of St Vincent and just before the Battle of Camperdown, when victories over the French and the Dutch respectively had given the Staffordshire potters two more themes for their pots—the sixty-year-old potter died, quite suddenly—'after only a few hours' illness,' says *The Times* obituary.

It seems likely that he was closely involved in the business right up to this time, for in the previous year very large capital investments had been made in new plant: John Pepper had been called in to design and erect new kilns and ovens, which not only brought down the fuel consumption—and with the continuing wars costs were rising steeply—but improved the distribution and constancy of heat in the ovens.

The Times went on to say that Josiah I 'possessed many amiable and endearing virtues, which rendered him an ornament to society and a service to mankind; in domestic attachments he was tender, generous and affectionate; in friendship faithful and sincere; nor was he less distinguished for charity and liberality to the poor; in short, he lived universally respected, and died not less generally lamented.' His grave in Stoke-on-Trent churchyard, round which traffic whirls busily today, near to those of both Thomas Whieldon and Josiah Wedgwood, describes him simply as 'Josiah Spode, Potter'.

31

Bone china dish stipple-printed in black with a view of a bridge over a river and a gilt border. Mark 'SPODE 557' in red.

Bone china beaker-shaped vase on high gilt foot, decorated with chinoiserie *of peony blossom below a wide border of emblems in panels and formal flowers with a background of eddies in colours and gold. Mark 'SPODE 868' written in red.* (Victoria & Albert Museum.)

Pair of bone china bulbous-shaped vases painted on either side with a bouquet of flowers in natural colours on a dark blue ground with gold scale pattern. (A larger companion vase has SPODE 1166 in red.)

One of a set of three bone china crater-shaped vases, painted with flowers in natural colours and gilt, the lower part coloured lavender blue.

Earthenware plate printed in black with views of Knypersley Hall, etc. in reserved panels in a blue ground.

(All Victoria & Albert Museum.)

Detail of oval stipple-printed dish opposite.

32

2. Josiah the Second:

(a) Felspar Porcelain and Stone China

The first few years of the new century must have seen great
activity, both in the factory at Stoke and in the London
warehouse. The new bone china had evidently been an
immediate success. The pattern books of these years show a
continual flow of new designs, samples of which would be
sent out with the country travellers or down to the Portugal
Street showrooms. They were aimed, one and all, at
shoppers who had hitherto been accustomed to look for fine
china in the newest modes at the Worcester premises in
nearby Bedford Street or at those of Duesbury of Derby in
Coventry Street, Piccadilly.

In the Stoke factory Josiah I's old Trevethick beam
engine, used for turning the grinding pans for flint, stone and
colours—and well in the van in its day—was replaced in
1802 by one of the new Boulton and Watt engines, a product
of the genius of James Watt. The works covered eight
acres and gave employment to 800 people.

Josiah himself had by now become a considerable mag-
nate. In 1804 he built a great house at Penkhull called The
Mount, whose vast range of stables and outbuildings was still
visible fifty years ago. There he entertained his fellow potters
and other professional people: Enoch Wood, himself on his
way to getting a vast fortune, enjoyed there 'the most
splendid and sumptuous entertainment I ever attended',
adding, characteristically, 'No intoxication.' Josiah II,
apart from his flute-playing, had become captain of the
Staffordshire 'Pottery Troop', a contingent of the county
yeomanry which had been founded in 1798 under the
threat of the Napoleonic invasion. This body undertook
'to render to our country at this momentous period every
service compatible with our situation in life', but, they were
careful to add, being busy men, 'only within the Limit of the
Pottery and Newcastle.' Business, in fact, was to proceed as

34

usual—in fact more so, for if the European blockade had cut the potteries off from a lucrative market, it had also cut the Europeans out of the English market, perhaps for ever.

In this prevailing mood of difficulties which were to be overcome rather than put up with, Josiah II set himself to look for even newer bodies, calculated to hit off the rapidly expanding market for ware of good quality but available at even lower prices than the bone china.

The firm had still been producing in quantity the earthenware of Josiah I's day. Somewhere about the year 1800, however, Josiah II began to look for a body which, though having a good deal of the refinement of his bone china, would attract another market, the one which was still importing 'Nankin' ware—as the Chinese export porcelain was then called: with Europe cut off this was now enjoying a boom on the English market. Here he would be offering a ware suitable for the large table services decorated with family coats-of-arms—the 'Chinese Lowestoft' or 'Armorial Lowestoft' as later collectors have called it, mistakenly,

Covered bone china inkpot in the form of a melon on a stand of four leaves with curved stalk and a coloured applied flower for a knop. Reliefs of berries and foliage in lavender blue slip. No mark, but colouring similar to that of a marked Spode jug. (Victoria & Albert Museum.)

35

owing to an error in attribution in the nineteenth century. Josiah knew that if he could only get the body right, he had plenty of resources for giving it the kind of decoration it needed.

After many trials he found what he was looking for by increasing the proportion of felspar in his bone china formula. China stone contained only 30% of felspar; and by replacing some of this with rock felspar he was able to fire the mix at a higher temperature and thus give it approximately the strength of hard-paste porcelain, but with much less brittleness and consequently fewer losses in the kiln.

Another of its advantages was that the softer glaze absorbed the enamel colours so that these no longer stood out in relief on the surface, where they were liable to flake off with wear, as often happened with the Chinese product. Spode was also careful to round off his edges: the Chinese ware had a rough and rather unsympathetic 'feel' in this respect.

Covered bone china sauce tureen and stand, with moulding of floral ornament in slight relief, and sprays of flowers and butterflies in panels in natural colours, also borders of bright coloured birds and gilt twig handles. Mark 160 painted in gold. (Victoria & Albert Museum.)

Teacup and saucer in bone china with formal gilt foliage outside, and wreaths of flowers in natural colours against a gilt background both inside the cup and on the saucer. No mark. (Victoria & Albert Museum.)

Bone china fruit basket and stand, with lattice work piercing picked out in gold; flowering prunus branches in 'Japan' style are painted on the bottom of the basket and small flowers in a diaper on the rim: twig handles. Mark double circle in blue and 282 in gold on its pair in red, also SPODE impressed. (Victoria & Albert Museum.)

The new body was again an immediate success; and once again the 'china-men' and the Town flocked to Portugal Street to place orders and choose patterns. In many cases they came to buy replacements or extensions to their existing services—which they could do much more cheaply by coming to Spode than by sending an order to far-off Canton. The decorators there, in any case, were sometimes liable to get instructions terribly wrong: they once turned a family motto of 'I think, I thank' into 'I stink, I stank'. At Spodes', of course, they had only to leave a pattern to be sure that it was copied faithfully and intelligently—and

above all quickly: orders sent to China might take several years to complete.

Some outstanding services survive from these days, and parts of them often come up for sale. Diners at the Gold-smiths' Hall still eat off Spode china emblazoned with the arms of the Company—which include the leopard's head familiar to all silver collectors—although their once notable service is no longer complete.

Thus was born 'Spode's Felspar Porcelain', destined to be made throughout Josiah II's career, and proudly bearing a mark which included the Union wreath—the rose, the

Bone china teacup and saucer, painted in natural colours with wild roses inside and outside the cup and on the rim and centre of the saucer, with gilt edges. Mark 'SPODE 3157' written in red.

Bone china teacup and saucer, moulded with flowers in slight relief; on the front of the cup a view of a cottage, in the middle of the saucer a river-scene painted in colours; gilt edges. Mark 'SPODE 1926' written on the cup in red, on the saucer in purple.

Bone china plate decorated with a 'Japan' pattern of conventional flowering plants and fencing within a formal border in red, blue, green and gold. Mark '967' and 'SPODE' written in red.

Beaker-shaped bone china spill vase, painted with large sprays of flowers in natural colours against a gilt background. Mark 'SPODE 711' written in red.

One of a pair of bone-china covered vases in Japanese Imari style with square bodies, angular gilt handles, painted with conventional flowering plants in red, green, pink and gold in panels separated by wavy vertical bands with gilt foliage on a dark blue ground.

Bone china vase, with gilt handles springing from lion's masks and bead ornament in relief round the rim and base, painted on either side with a bouquet of flowers in natural colours on a dark blue ground figured with scale pattern in gold, also with reserved rosettes in white and gold. Mark 'SPODE 1166' written in red.

(All Victoria & Albert Museum.)

thistle and the shamrock. For decoration, there were fine enamel colours—green, yellow, blue, orange, rose, brown, purple in various tints and shades. Gilding was used where appropriate; although sometimes, perhaps for better colour harmonies, perhaps for economy, this was replaced by an old gold colour.

Having secured this market—the gentry, the professional classes, prosperous tradespeople like himself—he now turned to a third one. This was the rapidly expanding lower middle classes, the small tradesmen, the yeomen farmers. He wanted a ware which would be as like the felspar porcelain as possible, but which would be cheaper to produce and have even greater strength and durability. In this market large families wanted wares which would endure a lifetime—several lifetimes—of washing up and packing away in their cupboards.

He found it by moving over towards the earthenware side of his range. Translucency was no longer the point: the ware could be as opaque as one liked; but it had to be earthenware of much greater strength and yet have a body which would take fine decoration either by painting or by transfer printing. Again felspar was his standby; and it gave him his 'Stone China', an extraordinarily dense body, with the 'ring' of porcelain and the faint bluish tinge of the Nankin ware. This shade was later changed: it went well enough with the blue transfer printing, but not so well with colours; and a few years later saw the 'New Stone China', in which potash felspar in place of soda felspar allowed the ware to vitrify more slowly and thus reduce the tendency to absorb smoke in the kiln.

For the third time Josiah II had scored a great success; and soon other potters were coming out with their own versions of this immensely hard, almost indestructible, but extremely handsome ware. Like Spode, some used the term Stone China, others such names as Iron-stone porcelain: perhaps the best-known of these latter, produced about 1813, was the famous Mason's Ironstone.

2. Josiah the Second:

(b) Printing and Painting

It is time to look at the decoration used on these various bodies.

Both Spodes, father and son, were able to command fine painting when they required it; but there seems no doubt that the swift rise of the firm in the early years of the nineteenth century must have been due very largely to its mastery of another process, transfer printing, used either on its own or in combination with painting.

The story of this process as used on eighteenth-century porcelain and the later bodies of the next century has already been summarized elsewhere in this series, but we can hardly follow the Spode story without looking at it more closely.

About the time when Josiah I had gone to work for Thomas Whieldon, a certain Robert Hancock, a Staffordshire man, had found employment as a copper plate engraver at the Battersea enamel factory, where he produced designs for printing on the famous boxes and other wares made there. The process, which appears to have been invented by an Irish engraver named Brooks, involved, first, engraving a copper plate, then inking it and applying to it a thin tissue of paper: the impression on the paper could then be transferred to articles of any shape—much as a child transfers a coloured butterfly on to the back of its hand.

The Battersea factory ended its very short existence—it had been working for only four years—in 1756, and Robert Hancock, seeing the possibilities of the new process in the world of china, went first, apparently, to Bow, and then to the young and very vigorous porcelain factory at Worcester, taking with him many of the designs and the actual plates which he had used at Battersea. The process had also been taken up—whether independently or not is a matter of

Vase in bone china painted with a 'Japan' pattern in colours and gilt. (Victoria & Albert Museum.)

some dispute—at the tile factory of Sadler & Green at Liverpool, where one of the partners had also been associated with copper plate engraving for prints.

The first of the Staffordshire potters to make use of the process was Josiah Wedgwood, who, about the year 1762, had begun to send packloads of his new creamware along

Vase in bone china painted with white, pale blue and gilt flowers reserved in a black ground. Ribbed body and gilt handles. (Victoria & Albert Museum.)

Inkstand in bone china with two detached dome-covered inkwells, also an urn-shaped candle-socket, painted in 'Japan' style. Mark 'SPODE 967', a cross and three dots in red. (Victoria & Albert Museum.)

the roads to Liverpool, where Sadler & Green would print the required designs on them and send them back. As so often happens when new industrial processes are introduced, the innovation was viewed with mistrust; it was feared that it would mean unemployment for the painters. There had in fact been trouble in the early days at Worcester and elsewhere. Even Wedgwood, as we have seen, after using the Liverpool printers for twenty-five years, still hesitated to do complete printing in Staffordshire itself: until 1805 he contented himself with printing the outlines of crests and shields for the painters to fill in. His son—another Josiah II —wrote to him: 'Painters refused to work, being disgusted, I do not know how, at printing'; and a few days later, having had a reply wrote: 'I had said to the painters just what you now direct me to do—that printing would be their best friend.'

It is said that William Adams of Cobridge, a member of

another of the great potting families, was the first to carry on blue printing over the glaze—in the original Worcester and Caughley manner—in Staffordshire itself. This was in 1775: but so far nobody had attempted to introduce there the underglaze process, with which Worcester and Caughley had later captured a profitable market: the last-named factory, of course, had sold them in the very Salopian Warehouse which the Spodes were to take over in 1784.

About the year 1781, however, Josiah Spode I took the plunge and brought into Staffordshire one of Turner of Caughley's own engravers, Thomas Lucas, together with the printer James Richards. A few years later he started to buy designs from Thomas Minton, who had engraved the original Willow Pattern for Turner of Caughley and was then a freelance in London. Minton—founder of the famous firm which still bears his name—came to Stoke and worked for Spode for a few years after his marriage in 1789.

Perhaps because the Spodes were keeping a wary eye on the labour situation, perhaps because they were anxious to continue to provide a range of coloured wares for their new bodies, the Spodes, from the very earliest days of their printing, made a speciality of combining the process with hand painting. Printing, after all, was basically a labour-saving device, a substitute for hand work: why not, then, use it to sketch in the general design, and then fill the colours in by hand? This would multiply and therefore cheapen output, make for more accurate drawing and at the same time—as Josiah Wedgwood had insisted—make *more* work for the painters, not less: moreover their labours were lightened since they were relieved of finicky detail and had only to work out harmonious colour schemes.

It was doubtless not lost upon the Spodes that by sweetening the painters in this way the firm could produce its unpainted monochrome printed wares without fear of labour upsets.

This combination of painting and printing was, of course, no new thing in English ceramics. At Bow, in the 1750s, there had been a class of Chinese subjects faintly printed in outline—presumably from engravings by Robert Hancock —with enamel colours over the glaze: they are attractive wares, but are inclined to have blurred outlines, perhaps because of the softness of the glaze. At Worcester too, after Hancock's arrival there, some of the printed wares were given washes of colour, perhaps by some outside decorator like Giles who had bought the pieces in the white with simply the printed design on them—a crossed swords mark

Bone china toy water can, with white and gilt reliefs on a deep blue ground. (Victoria & Albert Museum.)

had been added, presumably so that they could be passed off as Meissen. And as early as 1776, Josiah Wedgwood I was writing to his partner Bentley; 'Yes ... I have no doubt that painting and printing may exist together. I am fully convinced that the ivy and grape borders may be done at one third of what I now pay.' New Hall was also early in the field, using the combination on their hard-paste porcelain.

As with most processes, full success was not secured at Stoke at the outset. With the early pieces the black outline tends to show through the colouring; and some ingenuity was called for to overcome this defect. It seems to have been resolved by the choice of colouring materials, and the Spode pattern books give directions to the artists as to the colours to be used, of which there were six or seven. At first the colour painting was done very 'tightly', a kind of 'filling in', as in a child's painting book; but later, the artists left much of the transfer printing to speak for itself, simply adding judicious touches of colour. This method, when done with restraint, gave pleasantly free designs but in later years it was made an excuse for some rather crude work.

One of the best known of the early 'tight' designs is called 'Black Sprigs' (see Arthur Hayden's *Spode and his Successors*, facing page 74). It is given the pattern numbers 130–5, and is found filled in with two and three colours in green, blue, orange and brown. Another favourite, the famous 'Peacock' pattern, also appears in Hayden: it was No. 2118 in the Old Pattern Book—a jump in figures which reveals how many patterns were being evolved at this date.

Not all the outlines were in black: blue, biscuit and brown were also used. There are also stipple grounds—to be discussed later—combined with an outline design, and also a solid ground in a single colour—apple green or blue with transfer sprays and floral designs left in the white; they had the appearance of skeleton leaves and were apparently intended in many cases to be given white ornament in relief—presumably in the style of *bianco sopra bianco* on delftware.

47

Bone china pot-pourri bowl, with reliefs in pale blue lined with gilding. (Victoria & Albert Museum.)

Bone china pastille burner with pierced cover, the modelled flowers painted in natural colours, the cover and rim painted with a pattern of blue and green dots on a pink ground, and gilt scrolled edging. Mark 'SPODE 1506' painted in red. (Victoria & Albert Museum.)

'Tumbledown Dick' (see p. 16) is another of the very long-lived patterns dating from these early days: the first variations in the pattern books have the numbers 3018 and 3023. It is a charmingly simple design, thoroughly English in conception, showing a bird in a plum-coloured body with red and green wings, perched on a spray branch which stretches across the entire plain white ground of the plate, even climbing over the rims: the stump of the shrub is left in the original blue transfer printing. Later on more elaborate variations appeared: especially attractive are those with coloured grounds in which the transfer printing is used to give the crackled glaze effect of the prunus or 'hawthorn' patterns on Chinese ginger jars. One typical variation (No. 3715) has a deep yellow ground with the bird's body in Indian red and the wings in rich blue with outline gilding: another (No. 3803) leaves the ground in crackled glaze white.

A variety of other grounds was printed in this way. The popular 'parrot' pattern (see p. 16) appears on a vermiculated network ground, with passion flowers (No. 425): the painting is in pink, blue, brown, green and orange. A lobelia-blue network ground is also used as a base for brilliant painting of peonies, lilies and other flowers and sprays of leaves in yellow, pink, red, purple and green as pattern No. 3244: this appears on a pot-pourri jar with perforated cover and a wreath of honeysuckle painted inside.

Some of these early 'all-over' designs are not so successful. Hayden shows one (No. 3057) with a heavy grapevine pattern, the outlines in printed blue, with colouring in rich red and purple for the grapes, brown and green for the stalks and gold for the tendrils.

On earthenware the colours were sometimes applied not as enamels but on the biscuit under the glaze together with the transfer printing. It was possible because this body was fired at a lower temperature than the harder wares, thus enabling the colours to survive the intense heat of the kiln. One dish bearing the 'macaw' pattern (No. 429) has an outline printed in brown and five underglaze colours: other examples, however, may have as many as eleven colours—orange, pink, two tones of green, two of brown and four or five of blue.

Nevertheless Josiah II did not neglect to follow up his father's pioneer work in the matter of plain blue printing on earthenware. When Josiah I had started this process on the cream-tinted wares, he had taken as his first models the Chinese imported designs, or those developed by other potters like Thomas Turner of Caughley. But there were difficulties in adapting the work of hand painters to printing. Since they used only one colour they had to make the fullest use of tone values, and therefore aimed at making dramatic contrasts by fine or heavy strokes of the loaded brush. In line

Bone china basket-shaped trinket box covered with applied white florettes having yellow edges and red centres. Mark 'SPODE' painted in gold. (Victoria & Albert Museum.)

engraving, however, where light and shade had to be shown by cross-hatching or stippling, this was not so easy.

The early patterns show how real these problems were—and also how they were gradually overcome. In one of the early Spode willow pattern designs, for example, the central figures seem to be lurking in a cave; actually, the engraver has left a white space around them because he could not get sufficient tonal contrast to show up the figures. In the earliest of the plates, therefore, we get a flat effect, with a deeply cut design: moreover, these early pieces still use the formal

Bone china miniature ewer and basin painted in 'Japan' style. Mark 'SPODE' painted in red. (A very similar item bears the mark of the Herculaneum Pottery, Liverpool.) (Victoria & Albert Museum.)

Bone china toy basket, built of shells, on a green and brown rockwork base. Painted inside with flower sprays in natural colours. (Victoria & Albert Museum.)

Chinese border. This flatness was sometimes helped out by much suggestive use of white spaces, in the manner of Japanese prints. But this was not always appreciated by a public who by now wanted their wares well covered; the more engraving on the plate, apparently, the more they were prepared to pay for it.

A more effective way out of the difficulty was to bring into use another method of transfer printing, which appears to have been evolved at Worcester in the Flight and Barr era, somewhere in the 1770s. This was the glue-bat process, whereby an overall stippled effect could be obtained by using a sheet of glue and/or gelatine to transfer the design in oil on to the wares. It gave much greater delicacy of shading, and probably found its way into ceramics because of the current fashion for stipple printing in reproductions of the immensely popular and highly sentimental pictures by Angelica Kauffmann and Bartolozzi.

But printing was not only of great help to the engraver in producing tonal effects: it brought into being a new and much broader treatment which was, in fact, a long way removed in feeling from the original *chinoiserie*. On occasion it has a strong formalization and at the same time a highly romantic, almost barbaric touch: altogether an extraordinary kind of note to find coming from the most commercial of Staffordshire factories. In yet another style, stipple is the main feature, giving something like the effect of a theatre backdrop.

Whoever did these designs—and it is thought that a great many were engraved by the Bruce family, three generations of which worked at the factory—put power and imagination of no mean order into them. There is, as Hayden says, nothing in the Chinese original quite like the fantasy shown here, with cascades of blossoms and hanging fruit, rocks apparently lit from beneath, mysterious islands, magic shrubs and trees. These designs are usually called anglicizations of the Chinese: but in fact there is nothing very English about their mood: it seems much more to have been a half-remembered echo of the continental-inspired *chinoiserie* of the eighteenth century, which all these engravers would doubtless have absorbed in their apprentice days. Anyway there they are, a rich mine for the collector which has hardly yet been as thoroughly quarried as it might be.

So far as Englishness is concerned, nothing could be more English than a class of country themes which also appears in blue and white. There is a copper plate of the 'milkmaid' pattern showing a charming scene of a cow being milked in an open field by a kneeling girl: perhaps to this series also belongs the 'woodman' pattern, which could have been taken from a Kaufmann or a Morland original, or perhaps a combination of these.

Popular engravings were certainly the source of another large class of designs known as the Indian Sporting series. In June 1805 there began to appear the first of twenty monthly issues of a publication called *Oriental Field Sports*, or Wild Sports of the East, by Capt. Thomas Williamson: each comprised a printed story and two large aquatint prints engraved after drawings by Samuel Howett, a distinguished animal painter of the day. The venture was evidently very successful, for the parts appeared in 1807 as a bound volume which was later followed by a second edition. Hayden suggests that in copying these prints for his earthenware Spode was catering for the overseas markets, but it seems just as likely that they filled a need at home, where enormous interest was by now being aroused in the great Empire which had been won in India. A feature of these designs is the excellent vignette pictures around the rim—which also appear, quite illogically, in combination with other subjects.

Another popular series formed a kind of travelogue of views in the Eastern Mediterranean. They were based on engravings in *Mayer's Views in Asia Minor, mainly in Caramania*, published in 1803; from which the collectors generally call this the Caramanian series. Another series was based on views in Italy, usually of ruins or classical landscapes, from Merigot's *Views of Rome and its Vicinity*, a volume published in 1798.

Bone china iris vases, the outer two having a bloom with yellow standards and pink and yellow falls, the centre one with blue standards and puce and yellow falls, the leaves in tones of green. (Sotheby & Co.)

(Left to right) *Coffee-cup and saucer in the form of red and yellow tulip petals, the handle of the cup a gilt butterfly. Mark 'SPODE' written in crimson.*

Bone china porringer with cover and stand with applied gilt rose knop and twig handles, moulded in relief with rococo scrolled panels reserved on a ground of trelliswork, and over it an irregular lavender-blue border edged with gilt scrolls and small bouquets of flowers in natural colours.

Bone china chamber candlestick and extinguisher with wavy circular tray, gilt edged, painted with bouquet of flowers in natural colours on a pink ground. The candle-socket and extinguisher are modelled in the form of blue convolvulus flowers in natural colours, a looped stem forming the handles. Mark 'SPODE 4618' written in gold.

(All Victoria & Albert Museum.)

Most famous and long-lived of the patterns, however—it is still being made—is the 'Blue Italian'. It has not yet, I believe, been traced to any particular source, though it is obviously based on one of the many romantic classical landscapes so popular at the time. It fully deserves its fame and persistence, for it is a real masterpiece of its kind. By now the Spode engravers had really learnt their job, and the striking *chiaroscuro* effects in the painted Chinese subjects are here far surpassed.

Mr Sydney B. Williams, who first traced these designs to their source in company with another collector, Mr Gresham Copeland, shows many of them in his *Antique Blue and White Spode*, published in 1944. He grouped them into classifications and offered many useful speculations about them: he also reprinted a list of pattern names and dates compiled and published in 1878 by Llewellyn J. Jewett in his standard *Ceramic Art of Great Britain* (1878); and as both of these books are out of print it seems worth while giving it again here.

1806	Castle
1812	Roman
1813	Turk
1814	Milkmaid, Dagger Border, Tower, Peacock, New Temple
1815	New Nankin, New Japan, India
1816	Italian, Woodman
1817	Blossom, Pale Broseley
1818	Waterloo, Arcade
1819	Lucano, Ship
1820	Panel Japan, Geranium, Oriental
1821	Font, Marble
1822	Bud and Flower, Sun, Bonpot, Union
1823	Double Bonpot, Blue Border Filigree
1824	Image, Persian
1825	Etruscan, Bamboo
1826	Blue Imperial, Union Wreath

Jewett does not give the sources of his information, however, and although some of the dates can be confirmed from the discoveries made by Mr Williams and Mr Copeland, they do not always follow the particular succession one might have expected. The 'Turk' pattern, for example, suggests the Caramanian series, but 'India' in 1815 seems late for the Indian Sporting series which were popular as prints ten years before. The naming of patterns, however, was a pretty casual affair at that time; the term is more likely to have been used in its sense of the 'Indian flowers' of the Chinese porcelain brought in by the East India Companies—a frequent misconception as to origin. The 'dagger border', to judge by Mr Williams' illustration, is a design of the willow pattern family with a cresting border: the willow itself does not appear. Perhaps it is the one described here as the 'Temple'. Josiah I's first version of this had shown only one man crossing the bridge: now we have the more usual three persons chasing each other in accordance with the popular but certainly apochry-phal legend and rhyme. The 'Pale Broseley' is another of this family.

The 'marble' or 'mosaic' pattern was a fairly literal translation from the Chinese, using the famous cracked ice or 'hawthorn' theme—already seen in the one version of the coloured 'parrot' design. The pattern name 'sun' may possibly refer to a design with a round central decorative feature which is surrounded by the 'hundred antiques', well known in the work of eighteenth-century factories. The 'Waterloo' seems to refer to a design—probably one of a series—with a scene at the famous battle surrounded by emblems of victory, a rare excursion of the Spodes into contemporary events. The plate at the works bears the Copeland & Garrett mark.

There is a simple but attractive design of a geranium with an imbricated border which may well be the pattern described by Jewett under that name. The 'font' may be the design now known to collectors as the 'Warwick Vase', a well-known subject in pottery; it shows the great marble urn in the grounds of Warwick Castle. Here a design is given (for once) a highly appropriate border in the flowing foliated style of embossed silver. Another rare departure of Spode's into unaccustomed fields is surely the one described by Jewett as the 'Etruscan', a design crowded with classical vignettes in the Wedgwood manner. A simple border round a plain white plate is marked 'the Persian' and may be the one mentioned by Jewett. But there are many patterns and many variations of them: and it may safely be left to the collector to find his way among them and perhaps turn up new information.

One charm about all this blue and white ware is that one is still quite as likely to find it lurking in the junkiest of shops as anywhere else: I have done so myself, acquiring four of the Caramanian plates only quite recently for ten shillings apiece. The moral is, of course, always look through any pile of kitchen plates, however unpromising they or their environment may seem.

A word should be said about Spode borders. In the Caramanian series they are very nicely contrived, miniature themes from the subjects being placed around the rims, thus admirably heightening the general interest of the design: it almost seems as though the engravers of the plates were so entranced with what they found on the prints that they could not bear to leave anything out. I have an example, for instance, of the combination already mentioned, whereby vignettes from the Indian sporting series surround one of the Italian views. From the illustrations shown in Mr Williams' book this appears to have been common practice: one wonders what the users made of boar-hunting scenes in India alongside scenes of tombs in Asia Minor or classical ruins in Italy.

A modest interlaced line border seems generally to accompany the 'Tiber' pattern but there are also some with thoroughly English flowers or fruits, perhaps with a dash of Chinese diaper work. In the Willow pattern one finds, of course, very distant cousins of some of the old Chinese themes, like the *t'ao t'ieh* masks and the fretted 'thunder-cloud' patterns; while sometimes there is a very close attempt at a literal translation.

On the whole, Spode borders are a great deal more rational and appropriate than those of many other makers of blue-printed ware, to many of whom the wildest incongruities were second nature. Moreover one cannot but be struck by the extraordinary care taken—after the initial stages—in the way the different parts of the design, each of them on separate pieces of paper, were fitted together on the many and varied shapes of the wares. There is no doubt that, in their class, these Spode's blue-printed wares represent some of the finest craftsmanship of the day, and are worth every bit of the collecting attention paid to them.

Sucrier in felspar porcelain marked as below.

Teapot in felspar porcelain with applied white and gilt decoration on a dark blue ground and panels of flowers in natural colours at spout and handle. Mark 'SPODE 4896' and 'Spode Felspar Porcelain' in gold supported by emblem of the rose, thistle and shamrock. (Both Victoria & Albert Museum.)

59

2. Josiah the Second:

(c) Spode 'Japans'

One usually associates Derby with the vast range of colourful and richly gilded 'Japan' patterns which came out in the early years of the nineteenth century. There is good reason to believe, however, that Josiah Spode II was the first to issue a great many of these; and that he was followed by other potters as soon as they saw what a profitable market he had tapped.

Pieces from a dessert service painted with flowers and foliate design in colours and gilt. (Sotheby & Co.)

The earliest of these designs, from all the factories, were very pleasing adaptations of the Japanese Imari and other styles, but as they found their way on to cheaper wares, crowding and distortion often made them not only meaningless but downright vulgar. The unfortunate Robert Bloor, the Derby manager who took over that factory on the death of the last Duesbury, tried to rescue the firm by mass-producing a great many of these, but succeeded only in driving it into greater difficulties.

If we can go by the watermark numbers, the Spodes were in the field very early with their pattern No. 967, shown in Hayden (facing page 118), which has plenty of white china surface, and is a very pleasing effort. It is noteworthy that many of the themes used in this class of wares were not Japanese at all in origin, but Chinese, thus reflecting the continued interest at the factory since as far back as the days of Josiah I's first essays with outline printing. Pleasing as many of the designs are, however, as time went on Spodes did sometimes fall by the wayside and give their 'Japans' rather heavy-handed treatment in the way of crowding and over-lavish gilding.

From the point of view of craftsmanship, of course, this was all extremely skilful work, and such fine work will probably never be achieved again. This is especially true of the gilding, which has been very reasonably claimed to be the best of its day.

The earliest gilding on china was done with gold leaf, which was not only costly but was liable to wear off in use. At Chelsea, the French system of honey gilding was used, and it shows magnificently in the grounds produced there. In this process the gold leaf was ground with honey and oil of lavender, and the solution was then painted on and fixed by firing, a highly skilled craft. About 1790 a new process came in, whereby grain gold was mixed with mercury, the latter being evaporated off by firing. It left a gold film on the surface which could be burnished up to brilliance.

Josiah II was apparently the first Staffordshire potter to

apply this method to bone china. His chief gilder was Henry Daniell, who seems to have been an innovator of great resource. Apart from the solid burnished gilding, he introduced a matt technique for handles, knobs and other raised surfaces, and developed the process so that a raised gilt surface could be put on by applications of a white composition and tooled.

From the ledgers of 1810 one may get some idea of the strange articles produced at this time. They include punch bowls, mugs, sugar boxes, 'twiflers' (sometimes described as 'covered water twiflers'), butter tubs and stands, roll trays, supper plates, broth bowls, custard cups, toast racks, spouted tea tasters (for the professional tea buyers of the East India Companies), root dishes, salad bowls, chicken tureens, steak dishes, cheese stands, and dishes, 'turule' pans, strawberry baskets, cheese toasters, radish trays, match pots, snuffer trays, artichoke pots, asparagus trays, ice pails, sandwich sets, candlesticks with extinguishers, scent jars, inkstands, pen trays, wafer boxes, chestnut vases, 'hookays', syrup pots, card racks, cylinder pin cases, snuff boxes, rouge pots and violet baskets.

Josiah II died in 1827, master of a large business and fortune, the lists of the bequests in his will running to twenty-eight pages. William Copeland had also died in the preceding year, so of the London partnership, there survived only the latter's son, William Taylor Copeland. He now took over the management of the London business and the Stoke pottery in the interests of the executors of the estate and later of Josiah II's son Josiah III. The latter was never a potter, and in any case survived his father by only two years.

It was thus that the succession of the pottery moved from the Spode family to that of the Copelands, where it remains today.

Transfers of a copper plate showing a version of the Willow pattern, with the printed mark 'SPODE'.

SPODE

(1)

Spode

(2)

1 and 2, impressed marks used from 1770 onwards, sometimes also with pattern marks.

SPODE
2417

(3)

1989

Spode

(4)

SPODE

(5)

3 and 4, marks painted or written in various colours, with pattern numbers from 1790 on; 5, mark printed, usually in blue, from c.1784.

Spode

(6)

(7)

6, *Mark printed in blue, c.1790-1800; 7, printed in blue or brown c.1795-1805.*

Stone-China

(8)

Stone China

(9)

(10)

8 *and* 9, *Mark printed, usually in blue, from c.1805; 10, impressed mark on stone china, c.1810-1815.*

(11)

SPODE
Felspar Porcelain

(12)

(13)

11, *Mark printed in puce, gold or purple, c.1800-1833; 12, printed in blue, c.1800-1833; 13, printed in blue, from 1810.*